CARMELITE MONASTERY
LIBRARY
SARANAC LAKE, N Y

THE RISEN CHRIST

THE RISEN CHRIST

CARYLL HOUSELANDER

CARMELITE MONASTERY
68 FRANKLIN AVENUE
SARANAC LAKE, NEW YORK

SHEED AND WARD NEW YORK

© 1958 Sheed & Ward, Inc.
Library of Congress Catalog Card #58-5883

NIHIL OBSTAT:
Thomas J. McHugh
Censor librorum

December 12, 1957

IMPRIMATUR:
✠Jerome D. Hannan
Bishop of Scranton
Scranton, December 16, 1957

The nihil obstat and the imprimatur are official declarations that a book or pamphlet is free from doctrinal and moral error. No implication is contained therein that those who have granted the nihil obstat and the imprimatur agree with the opinions expressed.

Manufactured in the United States of America

CONTENTS

CHAPTER ONE

RESURRECTION

Our Christ-life is the life of the Risen Christ.

We know what the Incarnation means to us, that God the Son, by becoming man, caught up our human nature into his, made each one of us one with him. He took our human nature for his own and gave us his. He experienced everything that we do, excepting sin, and he even took upon himself the guilt and punishment of sin.

He made himself subject to our limitations: to discomfort, poverty, hunger and thirst and pain. He knew fear, temptation and failure. He suffered loneliness, betrayal, unrequited love, utter desolation of spirit, the sense of despair and death. He suffered all these things, and all the secret, incommunicable things known to each individual, which can never be told; and he overcame them all.

He overcame even death, and came back to the world bringing it life and peace and joy.

Christ seems to have fallen in love with our suffering, so passionately has he laid hold of it and made it his. He is known to the whole world as the Man of Sorrows. Yet he came to give us life, life full of joy. It was not with our suffering that Christ fell in love, but with us. He identified himself so wholly with our suffering, because our lives are necessarily made up of it. It is the inescapable consequence of sin. No one can escape it; everyone must somehow either make friends with suffering or be broken by it. No one can come close to another, let alone love him, without coming close to his suffering. Christ did far more, he wed himself to our suffering, he made Death his bride, and in the consummation of his love, he gave her his life. Christ has lived each of our lives, he has faced all our fears, suffered all our griefs, overcome all our temptations, laboured in all

2

our labours, loved in all our loves, died all our deaths.

He took our humanity, just as it is, with all its wretchedness and ugliness, and gave it back to us just as *his* humanity is, transfigured by the beauty of his living, filled full of his joy. He came back from the long journey through death, to give us his Risen Life to be *our* life, so that no matter what suffering we meet, we can meet it with the whole power of the love that has *overcome* the world. "I have said this to you, so that in me you may find peace. In the world, you will only find tribulation; but take courage, I have overcome the world" (John xvi.33).

He has come back as spring comes back out of the ground, renewing the earth with life, to be a continual renewing of life in our hearts, that we may continually renew one another's life in his love, that we may be his Resurrection in the world. We are the resurrection, going on always, always giving back Christ's life to the world.

In every life there are many secret resurrections. In our sin, we are the tombs in which Christ lies dead, but at the first movement of sorrow for sin he rises from the dead in us, the life of the world is renewed by our sorrow, the soul that was in darkness radiates the morning light. In the moment that we are forgiven, the world is flooded with forgiveness.

No wonder that the angels rejoice when one sinner does penance more than over the ninety-nine who need no penance, for the resurrection in the soul of the sinner is complete. It is not just the poor sinner licking his wounds and limping on, crippled by the past; it is Christ risen, alive, whole.

All day long, all over the world there is resurrection. A puny infant is baptized; Christ lives again, strong in his new life. A convert is received into the Church, a little appalled and disappointed by the sense of emptiness in his own soul, after the long tension of his conversion; Christ comes back to the world. A boy murmurs the monotonous story of his sins in the cramped confession box, the words of absolution are spoken; Christ lives again in the heart of mankind. A forgotten old woman dies in the workhouse. To those who close the eyes and cover the quiet face nothing extraordinary has happened; in the eyes of the Eternal Father, Christ has risen again from the dead.

Every day thousands of people receive Holy Communion. Christ who has been sacrificed on the altar is laid in the tomb of their hearts. There is no place where he will not come: prisons, hospitals, schools, camps, ships at sea, cathedrals and little tin churches; he comes to them all. He comes into the houses of the sick and the dying, regardless whether they are mansions or slums.

He comes to all kinds of people, from little children at First Communion, who bring him their first tender acts of love and reparation to be myrrh and aloes on his wounds, to old sinners who open their empty hearts to him hurriedly, at the last minute, just as Joseph of Arimathea's empty tomb was opened hurriedly, at the last minute before the Feast, to receive his crucified body.

Every day crowds of unknown people come to him, who feel as hard, as cold, as empty as the tomb. They come with the first light, before going to the day's work, and with the grey mind of early morning, hardly able to concentrate at all on the mystery which they themselves are part of: impelled only by the persistent will of love, not by any sweetness of consolation, and it seems to them as if nothing happens at all. But Christ's response to that dogged, devoted will of a multitude of insignificant men is his coming to life in them, his resurrection in their souls. In the eyes of the world they are without importance, but in fact, because of them and their unemotional Communions, when the world seems to be finished, given up to hatred and pride, secretly, in unimaginable humility, Love comes to life again. There is resurrection everywhere.

Our Lord has told us how we are to lead the Risen Life, and he has shown it to us. In his last discourse to the apostles he has told us. In the forty days on earth after his Resurrection he has shown us.

It is to be a life of love, love that creates, love that fills up the measure of each life with joy. Love that is light and peace. Love that forgives and heals and sustains, that makes us one. Love that gives life to the world and gives beauty to life. Love that is food and clothing and water for thirst. Love that is bread.

It is the love of the Eternal Father for his only Son, given to us, and it is given to us for ourselves and for one another.

"And I have given them the privilege which thou gavest to me, that they should all be one, as we are one; that while thou art in me, I may be in them, and so they may be perfectly made one. So let the world know that it is thou who hast sent me, and that thou hast bestowed thy love upon them, as thou hast bestowed it upon me" (John xvii.22-24). This love is not something insubstantial, to be lived only in the spirit. Christ chose a human body as the means to give us God's love. He gave us his body in his baby-hood, his childhood, his growing from childhood to boyhood, from boyhood to manhood. He gave it to us in his labours, in the stretch and pull of his muscles, in the sweat on his face, in his beautiful artisan's hands.

He gave it to us in the delight of his senses, in eating and drinking and sleeping, in his fasts and his vigils, in his weariness and in his rest. He gave it to us in his dying on the cross, and in lying dead in the tomb; and when he came back from the tomb, it was not a ghost who came back, it was the same Christ with the same body, risen and glorified.

In his glorified body, Christ was not any longer subject to human limitations. He could have compelled all men to believe in him by appearing from end to end of the earth, and showing them his glory. He did not need to eat or to travel on foot; there was no longer anything that could restrict him.

Before the crucifixion he had always kept his divinity secret until he had first won men and brought them close to him. He would not prostrate them with fear, they must not be afraid to live intimately with him and learn from this what God's love is. But now, since that little handful who did love him had been scattered and broken by the bewilderment and terror of the crucifixion, since everything for which they had in spite of recent failure given their lives seemed in ruins, would it not have been consistent with his mercy to have shown his glory, to have shaken his enemies, and to have restored the courage and joy of his apostles in a single glorious moment?

There is no doubt that it was his will that his love should sweep round the world like fire, and now there seemed to be nothing to stop it. Before, his message could only go as far as his voice could carry it, his mission as far as he could go on foot, and even among those whom he could reach tramping the roads and preaching in the streets, the temple and the countryside, many hearts were shut to him and would not open to the joy he brought for them. He wept over them openly; his tears could not move them, his love was frustrated.

Resurrection

Yet, now in his glorified body, he remained in the same little district, he hid his splendour, he kept the wounds of his Passion, he walked and talked and ate with men. He seemed as intent on persuading them to realize that he was human as he had been before on proving that he was divine, and instead of appearing in dazzling light all over the world, he sent other people to carry the news of his Resurrection, people who were still afraid, who still had the stains of their tears on their faces, who were still broken by the grief and horror of Calvary.

He came out of the tomb and walked in the garden and on the road to Jerusalem, as if he was eager to lay hold of the substantial earth with the same blameless feet that had so lately been lifted from it and fastened down by the cold, heavy iron to the cross. He had loved the earth before, had loved its mysteries of seed and harvest; and he loved it still. The love he had come to give was love like the seed in the earth. Love that must go down again and again into the darkness, be buried again and again in the heart of man, to live again and again in the resurrections of innumerable springs. Christ who had died and risen from the dead would not approach those whom he loved from outside; he would not only be the voice in their ears, he would be the silence in their souls. He would be the life that quickens in darkness and flowers in countless millions of forms of beauty. He would overcome fear and sin and sorrow and death in the heart of everyone who would love him until the end of time.

He, in his sacred humanity, could suffer no more; he could not be wounded or die any more; his life had become peace, joy, the absolute power of consummated love; and now by a supreme expression of that love, which completely passes our understanding and our realization, he gives *us* that life of joy. He gives that joy and peace to be at the very heart of our suffering, to make suffering and joy, for us as it was for him, not two things incompatible with each other, but just one thing, love—and he gives us his own power of consummated love to use for one another, to comfort and heal and restore one another; even, in a mysterious sense that those who have really known sin and sorrow and love will understand, to raise one another from the dead. "Believe me when I tell you this; the man who has learned to believe in me will be able to do what I do;

nay, he will be able to do greater things yet" (John xiv.12).

The ultimate miracle of Divine Love is this, that the life of the Risen Lord is given to us to give to one another. It is given to us through our own human loves. It is no violation of our simple human nature. It is not something which must be cultivated through a lofty spirituality that only few could attain; it does not demand a way of life that is abnormal, or even unusual; it is not a specialized vocation. It is to be lived at home, at work, in any place, any circumstances. It is to be lived through our natural human relationships, through the people we know, the neighbours we see. It is given to us, if we will take it, literally into our own hands to give. It is the love of human lovers, of man and wife, of parent and child, of friend and friend.

It is through his Risen Life in us that Christ sends his love to the ends of the earth. That is why instead of startling the world into trembling adoration by manifesting his glory, he sent the woman who had been a sinner to carry the ineffable secret, and sent the two disciples who had been bewildered by their blind inability to reconcile Scripture and Calvary, and sent the friend who had denied him, to give his love to the world, and to give it as simply as a whispered secret or a loaf of bread. So is it that we, sinners, wranglers, weaklings, provided only that we love God, are sent to give the life of the Risen Christ to the whole world, through the daily bread of our human love. "It is not for you to know the times and the seasons which the Father has fixed by his own authority. Enough for you, that the Holy Spirit will come upon you, and you will receive strength from him; you are to be my witnesses in Jerusalem and throughout Judea, in Samaria, yes, and to the ends of the earth" (Acts i.7-8).

CHAPTER TWO

AS I HAVE LOVED YOU

It requires no courage to accept the fact that the joy of Christ's love is given to us in the mystery of his Risen Life, which is now our life, and that the very meaning of Christianity is that we are to increase the life of the world, by giving this love to one another.

But when we go on to consider *how* Christ loves, therefore how *we* are to love, then indeed courage is asked of us.

We think of the Risen Life in man as a summer of Christhood in the world, a splendour of flower and fruit, a harvesting of love; and so it is, but not unconditionally. Christ has told us himself what the condition is; that the seed must be buried, must be buried deep down in the darkness, under men's feet, under the weight of the earth. That it must be subjected to the winter, to the season of frost and iron, of long darkness and short light. That it must accept the preordained measure, the slow pace and long pause in the periods of growth. It is only on this condition that it can bear fruit.

It is only on the condition that Christ dies that he rises from the dead; it is only because he surrendered himself to death, that we can live the splendour of his Risen Life.

He has told us in words which can have but one meaning, that our love is to be like his: "Your love for one another is to be like the love I have borne you": again, "This is my commandment, that you should love one another, as I have loved you. This is the greatest love a man can shew, that he should lay down his life for his friends" (John xv.12-13).

"Like the love I have borne you"—we know what that is like; it is the love which was consummated on the cross. It is the love which accepted the Father's will which, in a mysterious, dark night of mercy, required the suffering of the Passion. Obedient love, obedient even to the death of the cross. Love which includes everyone, excludes no one, reaches from end to end of the world.

Such then is our love; it must accept God's will; in the obedience of Christ, it must be a dying to self, it must be given to everyone, to the whole world.

Obedience means the fullest possible surrender to God's will, the acceptance of his law as the irrevocable plan of our own lives, so that all our emotion and passion and tenderness are strengthened, restrained and made holy by it.

In the fact of loving at all, there is for us, fallen creatures, an element of suffering. We realize the frailty of those we love, the million evil chances that threaten them. We are haunted by the fear of loss, of parting. By a strange paradox, falling in love brings us a new realization of our own nothingness, our helplessness to do, even to be, what we would, for the beloved. Only the sacrament of matrimony in which in a mysterious way God re-creates two as one, in his own love, can overcome this nothingness. But we live in a world that is de-christianized, divorced from love's very self; so marriage, for most people, involves material hardship and self-denial if they would live in obedience to God.

The lover is like the craftsman: he has to give himself to years of discipline, of patient work and perseverance, in order to attain his skill. There must be countless new beginnings, the exacting process of habit-forming, with its repeated denials of self, until at last his mind and eye and hand work in harmony on the material that he knows, as he knows his own soul. Just so is the lot of the lover, who has life for his material, life that sin has twisted, so that it is like wood that is knotted and warped. Yet on this material he acquires the skill that makes the craftsman an artist and enables him to fashion his own life into a thing of sheer beauty, and not his own life only, but the lives of those dear to him. Inevitably, in the process, he will have enlarged and strengthened his heart and mind; his hand will have become sensitive and capable, his eyes will be the trained eyes that see the loveliness of the world, that others are blind to. His home will be the little house that is built upon a rock, which stands fast when the rains come and the winds blow and the houses built upon sand are swept away.

That which was said in prophecy long before Christ's coming is true of the poor man who loves with Christ's love in the modern world: "Thou hast given him a strong conquest that he might overcome." This hard conquest leads to the splendour and fruitfulness of the love that has overcome the world. Even in human things, the procession through darkness to light, through winter to spring, from the cross to the Resurrection, is manifest.

The dying to self which makes our love like Christ's is not selfless; selfless love would not be love at all; but it is the surrender of self in our love. It is the reverse of selfish love, which is, after all, only self-love. Many who imagine that they love are really concerned with nothing else but being loved. Their husbands, wives, parents, children and friends become their victims; their self-love is plaintive, possessive and suffocating. They depend on others, and demand continual reassurance and flattery from them. They do not manage to go out from themselves and to give life even to those of their own household, let alone beyond it to the ends of the earth: and *that* is our final problem.

Yes, we are to love everyone, to exclude no one.

The rich man must love the poor man, but the poor man must love the rich man. The white man must love the coloured man, but the coloured man must love the white man. The wise man must suffer the fool gladly, but (and how seldom it is said!) the fool must suffer the wise man gladly. We are to love those who hate us, and—which for many is harder— those who are indifferent to us. Most baffling of all, we are to love those whom we do not know, whom we shall never know on this earth. This intense, self-giving love is to be given to them.

When we think of who these people are, the mystery deepens: criminals, people in bitter temptation, people in ignorance, the homeless multitudes known by the dreadful name of "displaced persons," people in forced-labour camps—the newly-born and the dying, and many martyrs dying for their faith and ours whose names will never be known.

These are only a few of the people in the world, but we cannot think of them, and not long to reach them. We realize, when we consider the martyrs, how mediocre our own lives are. This comes home to us all the more, if we realize that they are giving *us* everything that they suffer, giving us their deaths. We are in the deepest imaginable communion with them. What they do belongs to us, and what we do belongs to them; we are one with them, because we are one Body in Christ.

Equally we are one with the sinners of the world, and just as we realize with shame that the martyrs give us so much and we give them so little, we realize with shame that sinners need so much and we give them so little, because we are sinners too.

But how can any one person, limited in knowledge, imagination, circumstances, as most of us are, reach out in love to these widely different people?

Only through a yet closer and more real identification with Christ. So far we have thought of how we can be identified with him in our love of one another; if we are to reach the whole world, we must be identified with him in his love for his Father. Those who are, are not content merely to accept the suffering that comes. They go out to meet it, inflict it upon themselves, not through any morbidity, but because Christ did so, in reparation to the Father, for sin.

None has ever understood this so well as young children have; they do not question it, they look on the crucifix and see what is obvious. The little peasants of Fatima, from whom Our Lady herself had asked for penance for the world, went thirsty in the blazing heat of the Portuguese summer. St. Teresa of Lisieux while still a child saved the soul of a murderer by her sacrifices.

Nothing is more unpopular with the world than voluntary suffering; many pious people are disturbed by it and condemn it as being imprudent, unbalanced, a source of pride. Possibly they are made to feel guilty by their lack of it.

The world has a utility mind, and sees no *use* in vicarious suffering. They have no objection to a woman starving herself to become slim, or someone giving up his butter ration in their own favour; in such things they see a purpose. But why should someone whose life is in any case very poor and simple deny himself harmless pleasures, which hurt no one? And worse still, why do hundreds of people who could be of *use* in the world shut themselves up in convents as cold as refrigerators, and there deny themselves proper food and sleep? Why do they not remain among other people and do something useful?

Mortification is too much like the broken box of

spikenard spilt upon the Lord's feet for his burial, to be understood by the utility-minded world.

If what Christ chose to do as the ultimate expression of his love, as his way to reach all men and to lift them up to his heart, was to die on the cross, then surely the children and the saints are right in making their way of love quite literally like his.

To grasp this, we must look up to see what is happening on the cross, in Christ's supreme moment, when his love is consummated. He is held still in one place by nails: no more errands of mercy, no more raising the dead and curing the blind by a touch. He who came to be the Word of God, telling his love, is dumb. He who is the water of life is parched, dried up with thirst. His spirit, which is the source of all the sweetness in life, is emptied out, abandoned, so it seems, by his Father. His heart, the only heart that *can* love all men, is broken and does not beat any longer.

After all, the instinct is a true one which leads the simple childlike people to believe that when they deny themselves—when they choose silence and hunger and thirst and cold and stillness, and perseverance in prayer when the soul is dry as dust, suffering, so far as they can, what their Divine Lord suffered—God sees Christ in them; he sees them as his beloved Son loving with ineffable love on the cross; and in him their love is effective.

In our communion with Christ on earth, we do reach each other through the span of the cross, we can love all men, known and unknown, through loving literally with Christ's love.

It would not be fantastic in our days to ask if love, to be *literally* like his, might not demand of us that we should actually die for one another, as so many have done and are doing. But how we are to die is God's secret for each. The sacrifice of self at the heart of each life, offered for the world to God, is a complete expression of the sacrifice of the cross.

Christ expressed his sacrificial love in everything he did in his life; his very birth was a surrender of himself to death. His every act was an act of the same love that was consummated on the cross.

St. John, the dearest of his apostles, the only one who dared to follow him to Calvary, was also the only one who was not put to death for him. Surely, no one knew better than he who recorded Christ's last words, the meaning of the love those words describe? The voluntary thirst of one is a cup of cold water for another; the desolation, another's hope; the death of one, another's life; and the life of one lived for God, the comforting of another's death.

There are many people today in forced-labour camps hidden away from the world. There, unknown, nameless martyrs most of them will die. The few who have escaped tell us that, of all their sufferings, none was so bitter as the sense of having been forgotten. But they are not forgotten; another unknown multitude, those who share willingly every day in Christ's suffering on the cross, are always with them. When there seems no comfort left, suddenly, minute miracles happen: a gleam of sunlight, a bird's song, a whispered word of encouragement, an unexpected hand-clasp; and they hope again. Some silly old lady somewhere, some little child in a distant schoolroom, is giving them the gentle solace of Christ's tender love.

Some people learn to love the whole world through the love of God; for them the way of sacrifice is direct and informed with joy.

Others learn to love God through loving one another.

23

It is at home, in the family, that we can all learn the lesson of sacrifice, the miracle of grace that seems useless to the world. The "Great Silence" of the cloister begins in the stillness in the house when some-one is ill, or the children sleep: the poverty and the dividing of Christ's garments, in the sewing, patching and dividing at home; and so on, all through the lovely folly of the cross.

The heart that has been exchanged for Christ's heart radiates from the love of its own children to all the children of God, because now it cannot fail to love the Heavenly Father himself as Christ loves him.

There are not two kinds of love in Christ, one his suffering love, the other his risen love; there is only one. It is part of the glory of his Risen Life that in this love, even on this earth, is the beginning of the answer to his prayer that we all may be one.

On the road to Emmaus, looking back at the long story of his Passion in prophecy, and forward at the longer story of his Passion in us, he saw the answer to his prayer.

"Ought not Christ," he said, "to suffer these things, and so enter into his glory?"

CHAPTER THREE

THE HIDDEN GLORY

It is an amazing fact that Christ's Risen Life was a hidden life. His glory was hidden during the forty days between the Resurrection and the Ascension; his glory is hidden in his Risen Life now.

The forty days, the hidden life in Nazareth, the hidden life in the world today, have a likeness which is a revelation of the consistency of Christ. He is "the Way"; the Way does not change; we are helped by this consistency to recognize him in his hidden life in ourselves.

The Risen Christ

After his Resurrection, Christ showed himself to his friends five times, which are recorded. But what was he doing, where was he during the rest of the forty days? We may guess that he visited many unknown people; he may have gone to the slums of Jerusalem, the prisons, the caves of lepers. He may have been suddenly among children, playing with them, not recognized for who he was, but not questioned either. But this is guesswork, St. John simply tells us that "there are many other miracles Jesus did in the presence of his disciples, which are not written down in this book. . . ." (John xx.30).

One almost forgets that Christ did work miracles on the occasions recorded: astounding though this is, one almost forgets that the Resurrection itself is the miracle of all miracles. Christ wove these miracles of his love so naturally into the occasion, that they seemed to be inevitable happenings. As he intended that it should be, it is easier to see that his love is marvellous, than that it was expressed in marvels.

One of the miracles of the Risen Life was on the sea-shore—Peter's netful of fishes. Poor Peter, how good it is that he proved to be so splendid a fisher of men, for he seems to have been a poor fisher of fishes!

Each time we meet him in the Gospel, stiff and weary from spending the long hours of the night in his little boat, we are told that he had caught nothing! There is no record of a catch without a miracle. No wonder that John realized at once *who* it was on the shore, when Peter's net filled!

Were the other fish, already glowing in the fire that Christ had kindled, also miraculous? We do not know, the incident burns so brightly with his love that the miracle is hardly noticed. It becomes insignificant beside the fact that the Risen Lord was concerned with whether his apostles had something savoury for their breakfast, and that he, God, still served them!

Some of the Fathers of the Church say that when Christ broke the bread at Emmaus, he gave his Body to the two disciples in Communion; in our life now that miracle is worked day after day, with just the same secrecy. It happens before our eyes in the hands of men; it is a thing of such glory that the tongues of angels could not speak aptly of it. Yet while we watch we see nothing. There is the wafer of un-leavened bread; it is changed to the body of Christ who is God; it looks, feels, tastes, the same as before. The Blessed Sacrament is so much part of our ordinary life that we hardly ever realize that we are involved in a deed greater than any miracle every day.

We know from John's words that besides these two miracles Christ did many others in the presence of his disciples. About these there is silence, no record of any of them. They remind us of another kind of miracle which Christ worked over and over again, of which there is no record—the work of his hands in Nazareth.

Of course Christ did not create the things that he made in Joseph's shop. They were the result of hard work, of patiently acquired skill, just like any other artisan's work. The miraculous element is that *God* could have to work to make anything—that he should have to get his skill like any other lad in the workshop —measure, calculate, learn to sharpen his tools; that a man, whom he had created, should teach him to make the first long, clean cut with the saw, and how to run the plane smoothly along the sweet-smelling, newly-cut wood. It is the strange thing that though the Son of God spent the longest part of his life making things out of wood, there is nothing that he made left in the world. There is no record of even a passing reference to one of his works.

If only this world could boast of a stool, a chair, a wooden bowl, a yoke for oxen, or any single thing at all, made by the hands of God, when God was a workman!

How beautiful, too, that treasure would be; what proportion, exactitude, what finish and purposeful beauty it would show: but there is nothing at all to show for Christ's working life!

Did anyone value his work; did his customers pick fault with it, haggle over the price of it, beat him down? All these things are hidden in the silence that keeps the secrets of Nazareth.

Silence, too, keeps the secret of those "many other miracles" of the Risen Life.

But there is another record of those forty days, which brings us the key of this secrecy: "He had shewn them by many proofs that he was still alive, after his passion; throughout the course of forty days he had been appearing to them, and telling them about the kingdom of God" (Acts i.3).

The lock into which this key fits is our own lives today.

He wanted to prove then, as he wants to prove in us now, that it was *he* who was still alive, with the same character, the same way of doing things, the same way of working. Those of his miracles which need not be made public to give glory to his Father he works in secret, with such courtesy, such secrecy, that even those to whom they prove his presence do not always realize that a miracle has happened at the time, but only afterwards and gradually and by its effects. Just such a miracle was the changing of water into wine at Cana; no one knew the moment when it happened, or who among the wedding guests had caused it to happen; only when they tasted the wine, felt the glow of it in themselves, and exclaimed how good it was, did they realize that a miracle had happened!

Such are the daily unobserved, unguessed miracles of grace, contrition, conversion, hope, forgiveness, love, taking place secretly in the human soul. Real miracles, which could not possibly happen were not the Risen Christ among us. Miracles which still "tell about the Kingdom of Heaven" that is still not of this earth but within us.

We must look for Christ in one another. It is not enough for us to accept *his* gift of himself to us in our own lives. That could more than satisfy *our* capacity for love, but is not enough to satisfy his. Just as he wants us through *his* love of his Father in us to give his redeeming love to the whole world, so does he want us to *accept* it ourselves from everyone in the world, from those of our own household and those far away who, in him, are one with us.

We shall perceive Christ in others only if we realize that he is *hidden* in his Risen Life; that we can discern him only with the eyes of faith.

One clue in our search is that he is working his secret miracles of love through workers who have nothing to show for their work, just as he has nothing to show for his work in Nazareth. It seems to these countless unknown workers that they have no mission in life, that their work is without importance. But the fact is that over and over again it is in just these people that the Risen Christ abides, hiding his glory in them, because it is only through such lives as theirs that he can reach those for whom he must work those almost unnoticed daily miracles of grace which prove that he is, indeed, "alive after his passion."

He says to us, as he said to St. Thomas: "Blessed are those who have not seen, and yet have learned to believe" (John xxi.29). We need this reminder. How often, to our shame, does the thought enter our mind that some of the congregation of our parish church, the rather eccentric old women among its regular communicants, and the rather exasperating ones who push past us into the confessional to tell the priest in a voice that is clearly audible outside that they have nothing at all to confess, are not the most obvious proofs of the indwelling of Christ! And, without a doubt, unless they are a very great deal more Christ-like than we are, they must feel precisely the same thing about us!

We must learn to see Christ in others with the eyes of faith, because the whole orientation of our will, in which is the secret of peace, will depend upon whether we *act* as if we did see Christ in them or not.

It is part of God's plan for us that Christ shall come to us in everyone; it is in their particular role that we must learn to know him; he may come as a little child, making enormous demands, giving enormous consolation; he may come as a stranger, so that we must give the hospitality to a stranger that we should like to give to Christ; he may come to us in his Passion, disfigured by our sins and all sin, asking the utmost courage of us, that we may not be scandalized and may believe. He may come to us as a servant and compel us to the extreme of humility which accepts his service, as Peter had to do, when he washed his feet, and as the disciples did with unquestioning joy, when he cooked their little meal on the sea-shore.

If we see everyone in our life as "another Christ" we shall treat everyone with the reverence and objectivity that must grow into love, and as a matter of sheer logic we shall accept whatever they bring to us, in the way of joy or sorrow or responsibility, as coming from the hand of Christ; and because nothing comes from his hand that is not given for our ultimate happiness, we shall gradually learn that the things they do, the demands they make, all are part of God's plan for us. Once that is understood we can never again feel completely frustrated by anyone, or lose the serenity of our minds by nursing a grievance. Neither shall we ever again miss a joy that should have been ours through another person, because we dared not give ourselves to it, bravely. Parting too will lose its terrible power to afflict us, even the parting of death, for there will be no one whom we shall not find again in him for eternity.

In the martyrs of today, those to whom we have a continual debt of faith and love, we know Christ as Thomas was taught to know him, by his wounds, by the stigmata of his Passion.

They too manifest the *hidden life* of the Risen Lord. Many of them are literally hidden. They are not even names to us, not even faces in a newspaper photograph. Hidden from sight, out of reach of ordinary human sympathy, they have even lost their identity—or rather, their only identity is Christ. In places where, but for them, he could never come, they are proving that he is still upon earth, alive after his Passion. By their living deaths they are proving that he has conquered death.

Others, like their Lord, are held up for the whole world to see; in them too his glory is hidden; they "have no comeliness whereby we shall know him"; they are wholly identified with his suffering: mocked, disfigured, covered in man's spitting. False witness is brought against them. They are crowned with thorns. To many people they seem to fail; through the means available to modern persecutors, their enemies can even destroy their minds. They must suffer Christ's

34

bitterest grief, the knowledge that their very martyr-dom may scatter their flocks.

Perhaps it is most difficult of all to realize, or to believe, that the Risen Christ is hidden in our own lives. Difficult not only for others, but for ourselves.

If his purpose in indwelling men is to radiate the light and heat of his love through the whole world, how can we honestly believe that he chooses people for such a mission who have no great talents, no work of importance, nothing to show for the work they have done, and no influence; people moreover whose circumstances, humanly speaking, are, by God's own will for them, both cramping and inescapable?

But it is precisely from such lives that his love can and does radiate. We know nothing about the "many miracles" which were not written down. But what we do know of what things he did and how he did them in his Risen Life, shows us that the power of his endless miracle of love *is* given to the most circumscribed lives, and the means whereby it is worked are means that belong to us all. Words, a human voice, sympathy, hands to serve. These are the conspicuous means Christ used—these and, judging by that last netful of silver fish for Peter the Pope, a literally adorable humour!

He used these means to bring peace, to comfort, to give courage, to restore self-respect, to change fear to love, shame to joy. Look at the five recorded instances one by one to see the genius of his use of just our limited means.

To the stricken world in the person of Magdalene, compassion: "Why are you weeping, for whom are you seeking?"

To the apostles, his first word, "Peace!"

To Thomas, "Believe" because of the wounds— "the courage of faith."

To Peter, the wonderful opportunity to affirm his love.

To the disciples who mourned him as lost, communion with him.

The only condition for finding and recognizing the Risen Christ today is that we love him: not power, chance or virtue, but only love.

He "showed himself first of all to Mary Magdalene, the woman out of whom he had cast seven devils."

On the first Easter morning, that woman kept the

faith of all the faithful, for all the faithful, and no one would believe that she had seen the crucified Lord alive: "to their minds the story seemed madness, and they could not believe it."

May we, most of all when it seems madness, keep our faith in the Risen Christ unshaken in our hearts.

CHAPTER FOUR

REVEALING CHRIST'S LOVE

Christ never forced his love on anyone. Though he is perfection, he never allowed himself to dominate the will and mind of another with his own. He desired love that would be a communion, closer than human marriage, closer than the life of a mother to her unborn child, an unimaginable communion of love, but all were to come to it through their own experience, in their own way; even, by a positive miracle of mercy, through their own imperfections, through the experience of their weakness and need, through sorrow for their sins.

The impulse was to begin for each one in his own heart. It was never to be a violation of the individual soul; instead, a gentle, almost imperceptible, movement of inward life. It could be likened to the quickening of the seed in the earth, when the warmth and light of the sun which is burning in heaven comes down through the darkness and enters into it, and the tender green shoot pushes towards the light, compelled by the very sun that is so far away, and yet is within it.

In the five recorded incidents of Christ appearing in his Risen Body, he allowed each of those to whom he showed himself to discover that it was he in their own way, through their own medium. His approach to them, always exquisite in courtesy, miraculous in humility, was in each case one that showed his intimate knowledge of each one individually. He knew which would be the most natural way for that particular person to respond to his love, and what each needed to lift his or her heart from the sorrow or shame which was crushing it and restore it to the joy that would enable it to enter into communion with him.

To Mary Magdalene the revelation was a word of tenderness, and at the same time of restraint, followed immediately by entrusting her with the news of his Resurrection to give to his apostles.

A woman whose experience had been the opposite to Magdalene's—one who had lived a sheltered, protected life, a life of virtue, who had always been esteemed by her contemporaries, who could not even imagine what it is like to be held in contempt, to hold oneself in contempt, to be regarded even by those who love one as being capable only of emotionalism and instability—simply could not have understood the sheer glory it must have been to Magdalene to be asked by Christ for the pure, supernatural love implied by his words, following that intimate utterance of her name —"Mary": "Do not cling to me thus; I have not yet gone up to my Father's side" (John xx.17). And then, to be given a commission which could only be entrusted to one whom he knew to be level-headed and wholly trustworthy, and which was the final message of Christ's Incarnation and Resurrection to the whole world: "Return to my brethren, and tell them this; I am going up to him who is my Father and your Father, who is my God and your God" (John xx.17).

There was no proof needed for Magdalene other

than the stirring of life in her own heart in response to the illimitable courtesy of Christ's love for her; but it was otherwise with the apostles. Those amazingly incredulous men, who had been warned, who had had the prophecies that were to be fulfilled pointed out to them, who had been told that Christ would rise on the third day, who had actually seen him raise another man from the dead, were still unconvinced; they frankly disbelieved Magdalene and, as men are so apt to do when faced by the courage of a woman's love, they thought that she was, at least temporarily, insane. They were frightened, trembling for their own lives, bewildered by what had happened and by what might be going to happen, and they locked themselves up "for fear of the Jews."

Christ knew their need—their need for reassurance, for courage; that they must be calmed like frightened children: he knew the turmoil within them, like the tossing waves of the sea which he had once calmed with a word; so he came secretly yet wonderfully through the doors, and his first word was "Peace!" He knew too the smarting humiliation of their failure through weakness in his hour of need, and once again the genius of his human love shines out; they are given the power to forgive, to absolve sin, to strengthen and comfort the weak, and to reunite the scattered, frightened world of sinners to himself. "With that, he breathed on them, and said to them, Receive the Holy Spirit. When you forgive men's sins, they are forgiven, when you hold them bound, they are held bound" (John xx.22).

Quite different is his approach to the disciples on the road to Emmaus; these are scholars, they must come to the point of communion with him through the travail of the mind. Step by step he takes them back through the Scriptures, leading them to know him by thinking their own thoughts, by linking up the academic knowledge they have acquired in the past with the events of the day, and thrashing out the problem that is so baffling to intellectuals in all ages, the problem of suffering.

Through a totally different approach to the same problem he convinces Thomas. He well understands the refinements and mental conflicts of the thinkers, to whom, even when they suffer, suffering can still be contemplated in the abstract, and who are hard put to reconcile themselves to the idea of their innocent Lord suffering, of God dying. But he has no less understanding of Thomas, who is exactly the opposite: the poor man who has no philosophy to be armour against the wounds of the world, no thoughts to help him through the loneliness of his own anguish.

Just as the intellectuals could hardly believe that Christ would suffer and die, and keep wounds in his body as his one glory brought back to Heaven from earth, Thomas could not believe that it *was* Christ, if he did *not* do precisely those things, if he did not come to the suffering world with the wounds of it still wide open in his own body. It was when Thomas actually put his own hands into these wounds and felt, as it were, his own sins and sorrows redeemed in the glorious Body of Christ, that the cry came out of his heart: "Thou art my Lord and my God!" (John xx.28).

Last there is Peter. Who but Christ would have known that the one thing that could lift up that broken heart was not a formal act of contrition, but a spontaneous, almost an exasperated cry of love: who but he would have thought of provoking the same impulsive temperament which had made a coward of Peter with such cruel results, to give it the courage to break out into those acts of love? And, as it was with the

others, Peter is given something to do for Christ,
something that is exactly suited to his inmost need,
as it has been in the case of each of the others. He is to
become the shepherd. Christ shows him that he knows
what the sorrow for his sin has done to him, how it has
taken away his cowardice, so that he can give him even
this charge, the charge of the shepherd who is to pro-
tect the frailest of his flock, his lambs and his shearlings, to feed them, and if need be to give his life for
them. Could he give greater proof of his trust in the
reality of Peter's love, in the truth of Peter's word:
"Lord, thou knowest all things; thou canst tell that I
love thee" (John xxi.17).

Why we, who are members of Christ's body on
earth, his Church, *are* so, is a great mystery; there
cannot be a living Catholic who does not know a Prot-
estant, or a pagan, or an agnostic who does not seem
to him to be far worthier of our vocation, far better
endowed for it by nature, and even by grace. But the
fact remains that God has chosen us for the tremendous destiny of love, and if the wonder and the joy
of it is ours, so too is the responsibility of it. That
responsibility is to prove to those who are still un-
aware of it that Christ has risen from the dead and

that he is in the world now. We have to prove Christ to the world, and we have to prove him to the world by our own lives.

We cannot do this without a very close imitation of Christ's way with other people, and without surrendering our lives so wholly to him that he may act through us and gradually obliterate our own selfishness and stupidity by his love and understanding.

This is expressed perfectly by St. John the Baptist, who defines the true attitude for each of us, saying: "He must become more and more, I must become less and less" (John iii.30).

Christ "knew what was in man": that is the secret of his method; he knew and loved every man, objectively and individually, as a separate person, a unique person; he respected their otherness, their independence, even their slowness, their limitations, which were all part of the experience which was to bring them to the realization of his love.

Christ wishes to approach people through us today in just the same way, through just the same means, as he did in his Risen Life.

We, on the other hand, tend to use methods intended to convert not this or that individual but the whole world (as if the world were a hydra-headed monster). Usually these methods are arguments. We know that the arguments are unanswerable, and we tend to use them like a sledgehammer with which we deal blow upon blow upon the head of the unfortunate victim of our apostolic zeal, as if we could stun him into belief, and convert him by concussion.

Most people who want to know God and who are outside the Church have just one thing that is precious to them, though to us with our clear-cut definitions, our discipline and our sacraments, it may seem so vague that it is hard for us to realize how much it means to them. This is their personal approach to God. Very often it seems to be hardly that at all, so vague is it, so closely does it lean to sentimentality. It may be simply a memory of childhood, or a stirring of the spirit when a certain familiar hymn is heard; it may be just a fling of the heart to God, on seeing the first wild spray of blossom that proclaims the spring. But it is quite surely an indication of that individual's approach to God and of his approach to them, and it is as sweet to them as it would be to a blind man if, reaching out in darkness, he touched the garment hem of Christ.

Too often, through our own fault, we give people who are thus clinging to their own personal contact with God the idea that Catholicism would sweep it away. Quite wrongly, we give them the idea that we are not seeking any more, that we have a formula for everything, that we hold feeling in contempt, live only by acts of will, and that there is nothing that we cannot explain.

Of course this is untrue. We too are always seeking for God, always reaching out blind fingers to touch his garment, and we are blinded by the very light of the mysteries of our faith, which we can live by but cannot explain and can barely begin to understand.

To the enquirer, our hard, unanswerable arguments, dealt out blow by blow with our sledgehammer of zeal, are all too convincing—to the mind. But the heart rises up in revolt against "apologetics" which may convince against the will, and sweep away that lovely touch in the darkness which is at the heart of their lives.

When our friends come into the Church we sometimes tend to domineer them, to exert a too important influence, a possessiveness which is unlike Christ. We do not allow them the time for growth. Some of us persecute Christ's poor shearlings with our piety, we try to force our pet saints and devotions on them, even our eccentricities, and we do this with the same peculiar insistence with which many people continually try to persuade their friends to go to their own dentist! But the one real charity we could give to them is to leave them alone to listen in silence for "the still small voice" of God.

Christ's example shows us so clearly and simply how to practise his objective love, how to learn what is in the hearts of others. First we must realize everyone separately and approach each one differently.

There are some who come to him through their minds, through study, and through considering the problems of today, suffering above all. We should be ready to discuss their thoughts with them, not in order to score points against them in argument, but to help them to clarify their own ideas, to form their own conclusions—this, with the gentleness of Christ, that they, like the disciples on the road, may feel their hearts burning within them as the mystery of the Redemption begins to shine on their minds.

Not only by words or acts can we show Christ to men, but also by the quality of our love. Sometimes in denying ourselves its immediate delight—"Do not cling to me thus" (John xx.17); sometimes in the humility which causes us to put ourselves into the hands of the loved one: "Let me have thy hand; put it into my side" (John xx.27). Sometimes by serving, lighting the fires, cooking the food, in the simplicity of the Risen Christ. Sometimes by forgiving, with his forgiveness that heals because it asks only for love: "Simon, son of John, dost thou love me?" (John xxi.17).

Sometimes the revelation is secret, and is made through reparation, through gladly bearing the wounds of sin, our own and the world's, inwardly, and offering our suffering and sorrow in Christ's to redeem the world and bring peace and the forgiveness of sin. By this means it is that Christ in us still passes through the locked doors of other lives, of closed minds and frightened hearts. "The disciples had locked the doors of the room in which they had assembled; and Jesus came, and stood there in their midst" (John xx.19).

CHAPTER FIVE

THE PERSONALITY OF CHRIST

Christ was, and is, completely human, as well as being completely God. This is so astonishing a mystery that we cannot grasp all that it implies, even in practice, with our tiny understanding.

Without quite realizing it, many people incline to feel, if not to think, that the true nature of Christ, the nature of God and the nature of man, modified each other during his life on earth, and so gave his experience as a man a slightly different quality to ours.

When we remember his humanity, we are apt to

limit it to his body. We see the tiny body in the crib, the body naked on the cross. We know that the pain of the scourging, the cross-bearing and the crucifixion were real, because Christ was really human. But we reflect too little on his human soul, his mind as man, his emotions, his individuality, his temperament, indeed everything that makes up his human character.

It is startling, for example, to read that he "advanced in wisdom with the years" (Luke ii.52). That he had to grow in knowledge, learn from people, from environment, from his own creation. That he had to observe, remember, and relate the facts of his experience, like other boys.

He watched the birds, examined their nests, marvelled at the architecture which builds the home around the mother's breast. He went to collect the eggs in the farmyard, and noticed how the hen gathered her chicks under her wings. He observed that not only flowers were beautiful, but the grass that he brought in to stoke the oven. He watched the wheat grow, from the thin green spear to the reaping, probably giving a hand with the harvest and hearing the farmers talk of the tares in the grain, the sheaving and threshing and the rest.

He watched his mother baking bread, fascinated as any child by seeing it rise. He watched her bottling wine, patching old garments, sweeping her house, lighting the lamps; he went with her to draw water from the well.

Walking on the hills round Nazareth, he saw the sheep flocking to their shepherd's voice, and the young lambs carried in his arms.

He talked, as boys love to do, to the shepherds and to the fishermen down on the shore. He listened enthralled to the stories of shepherds who had given their lives for their sheep, and the stranger stories of the sea, told by the fishermen who were out all night in their boats.

So he "advanced in wisdom with the years" and gradually these things which were teaching him the wonder of created life were built into the whole plan of Divine Love in his human mind. Later on he taught others to know him and his Father by pointing to these everyday things, which often go unnoticed, or unrelated in our minds to the eternal mysteries of which they are symbols.

It was not only with his mind that Christ grew in knowledge; his emotions too responded to everything around him, so that when he came to teach the crowds, the images that he used were memories of his childhood and his mother's home, but the detached observations of the absorbed little boy were now charged with the burning love of the grown man.

He was leaven and light, he was bread and wine and living water, he was the good shepherd and the mothering bird.

It is not enough for us, if we live in Christ, to try to imitate what he did, we must also acquire his personality and grow to the maturity of our Christhood through the means by which he grew to his maturity of manhood, so that the trifling things of our experience, transitory by themselves as the fall of a rose, become charged with eternal meaning by the ray of his light.

It is not by chance that God's plan for our risen life is sacramental and that the substances which are the outward signs of the sacraments are also the simplest things used daily in our homes, reminding us hourly of the effects of sacramentals on our souls, and showing us how we are to "advance in wisdom with the years" by just the same quiet attention and response to our small worlds that Christ gave to his.

Water purifies and quenches thirst, oil softens, cleans, lubricates, and burns in our lamps. Wheat contains the germ of life and bread is life's mainstay. Wine warms, invigorates, feeds and uplifts us.

Every day, in our homes, we look on the invisible, handle the intangible, use the substances that Christ uses for Heaven's mysteries, and, performing the work of Martha, possess the key to Mary's contemplation.

It is God's plan, too, that the sacraments are given to us at the hands of men. Those who misunderstand God's tenderness for us boast that they need no priest. They "go straight to God." But in the most critical times in our lives, we are normally incapable of such an act of will. At baptism someone must pledge our souls for us. When we are dying, normally we need another human being to help and comfort us, to make our act of contrition for us, to be our voice in God's ears because once again we are inarticulate, to put the Holy Viaticum, the food for the journey, into our mouths for us.

Because Christ comes to us in human hands, just as he first came in a woman's arms, no one need ever be quite alone and without human help. He comes to the loneliest, to outcasts, degenerates, strangers, to prisoners and to men and women in the condemned cell, and comes to them all in the hands of a fellow creature who is led to them by the Spirit of Love.

Christ abides in each one of us, and in each one of us he waits to receive the human kindness of men. It is for us to allow it to him at last; even the greatest sinner, though he waits even until the hour of his death, does not only receive comfort for himself, when he opens his heart to the priest who absolves him, but he gives comfort to Christ!

No man was ever a more complete man than Christ —what we should probably call "integrated" now, but it would be the wrong word, as it implies having been disintegrated before, and Christ was always whole, always in perfect harmony within himself; but he realized and felt the insufficiency of any man by himself, as men are intended to be in communion with one another. He knew the interdependence of human creatures, and felt it himself both in little things and in tremendous ones.

As a human being he accepted the limitations of human beings, and discarded the false heroics. When he needed rest he sought it, though without complaining if he was disturbed or frustrated. He was not one of those disheartening people who, when they have exhausted their whole household by the endless fever of their activities, say, "If you want a thing done properly, do it yourself." He often delegated his work. He delegates it to us today, and this is not surprising because he has always chosen to entrust it to those who seem unsuitable as well as unworthy.

Because he was tired, he sat down to rest on the well in Samaria, and sent that rather tiresome woman who came to draw water, to convert a whole village. His own preaching and miracles never achieved what this apparently over-sexed woman did, when he was resting.

He wanted and asked for help and still more for sympathy. Simon of Cyrene *had* to help to carry the cross; Christ *could* not carry it alone. Christ intends no man ever to carry the cross alone.

We cannot remind ourselves too often that our life in the Risen Christ is an interchange between us of his love. In the power of his love in ourselves, we give to him in our neighbour.

There is nothing Christ asked for more urgently in

his earthly life than sympathy, nothing he asks for more often and receives less often in those in whom his Passion is lived today in its deepest humiliations and derelictions.

There are too many "commonsense Christians," afraid to spend themselves on anyone from whom they do not get visible results. They are ready with hard work for reform, they pour out good advice, they are proud to be realists who repudiate everything that seems to them to be impractical, including the poetry of Christ, but they have no use for those baffling human creatures who won't—or can't—play the game by their rules. These "realists" refuse to see that there are problems which cannot be solved, griefs which cannot be healed, conditions which cannot be cured. They are impatient with the suffering they cannot end; unable to accept its reality, they wash their hands of it, because they cannot, so they think, do anything about it.

But we cannot make an end of Christ's suffering, for as long as the world goes on, the Passion of Christ will go on in his members; and he will ask, not for his suffering to be mitigated, but for sympathy. In

Gethsemane Christ tried to awaken his apostles, not because they could take away his agony, but because they could give him their compassion.

Sympathy is real *self*-giving; compassion is only that, giving self to suffer in sympathy the thing that cannot be cured. That is why sympathy with Christ in those who suffer his Passion to the end is the rarest thing in the whole world.

Christ rose, bearing his wounds. There are "other Christs" today, who are not always recognized as such, *because* they carry a stigma—his stigmata. People who bear a burden of hereditary disease, or temperament or temptation, neurotics and "borderline cases" made helpless and dependent by affliction which at the same time makes them shunned by society. Mentally ill people, often neglected by their families and left to strangers to visit them in mental hospitals; old senile people who have outlived all whom they had a claim on and are unwanted; people who are outcasts and who are broken in mind and body by the wars caused by our habitual sins. In these people Christ asks only for compassion, that we shall be awake to his presence and to his suffering in them, and visit them in the redeeming sympathy of love.

The Personality of Christ

Christ refused the gall offered to him on Calvary to mitigate his suffering. But he did not refuse gifts which would scandalize the commonsense Christians, with their fear of extravagance and waste, gifts which expressed the sheer poetry of love and adoration.

He accepted the gifts of the Magi, useless to a little infant, inappropriate to a carpenter and his wife taking shelter in a stable.

Yet, what a picture that was of the world today, as Christ would have it to be! The frankincense mingling into the stench of the cattle-shed, the slums, the segregated neighbourhoods, the concentration camps of the world. The vicarious suffering which is myrrh in the precious casket of the dedicated heart. Rich men's gold at the feet of the outcast and the destitute. Wise men on their knees wherever Christ is born again in a human life.

He accepted the precious ointment poured over his feet for his burial, the gift of sympathy which could not save him from his Passion, yet brought him comfort which was almost festive in the beauty of its expression.

Christ in his humanness wanted joy. He chose to suffer completely and to the end, but he also wanted absolute joy; he wanted to receive it and he wanted to give it.

Nothing that mattered to a human being was trivial or unimportant in his mind; he was concerned about the possible embarrassment of the host at the wedding feast, and he changed water into wine to prevent it.

That first miracle was not done to cure affliction, it was done to increase joy. The occasion was already joyful, a wedding feast, but Christ brought more joy. That too was a perfect expression of his human character.

It is a great part of our Christ-life to increase joy in the world, just as it is. First of all in our own lives, for joy must be a reality, something as deep and still and pure as water in a hidden well, under the ground. The forced smile of the amateur Christian is a blasphemy.

We cannot increase joy unless we "put on" Christ's personality, and our own joy actually is his. People driven by the fiend of vanity who roameth abroad— not seeking whom he may devour but trying "to spread a little happiness," seeking with whom he may interfere—know nothing of true joy.

First of all its increase must begin in ourselves; we

must grow in wisdom as Christ did, by deepening our understanding of the sacramental life, through the very substance of every day. Until there is nothing we see or touch that is not charged with wonder for us, though it is something as familiar as the bread on the table. And there is nothing that we do, though it be no more than filling a glass with water for a child, which does not sweep the loveliness of God's sacramental plan through our thoughts, like a great wave of grace washing them clean from sin and the sorrow that is inseparable from it.

Then we can increase joy through compassion, even where there is incurable suffering, for if we even want to put on Christ's personality we shall radiate his light, and he is the light which shines in darkness, which darkness cannot overcome.

In matrimony, it is the bride and bridegroom who give one another the grace of the sacrament; and it goes on, as they grow together in one another's love, a gradual increase of joy, which nothing, ultimately, can take away from them. In a sense they are one another's priests, because their life is a lifelong giving and taking of Christ's life. Everything in their lives has a quality of miracle; all their words of compassion or forgiveness are in a sense little absolutions; their union a communion with Christ. Every breaking of bread at their table, a remembrance and more than a remembrance of him.

Human marriage is only a symbol, a shadow of the marriage of Christ with his Church, of the continual growing together in creative love, of the daily transformation of everything that so much as touches the hem of his garment; and it is *we* who are the Church!

By our baptism we are bidden to the marriage feast where water is changed to wine. Cana is an image of our Christ-life on earth, but Christ is not only a guest, he is the Bridegroom with whom we must rejoice, who desires for everyone who loves him "that my joy may be yours, and the measure of your joy may be filled up" (John xv.11).

CHAPTER SIX

THE PRAYER OF THE BODY

One is often asked the question: "Which do you think the harder to endure, suffering of mind or body?" It is a silly question, because everyone knows that physical, mental, and spiritual suffering too, are inseparable. Mind, soul, and body act and react together. In fact a man's capacity for physical pain is measured by the sensitivity of his mind. The great criminal anthropologist Lombroso, who made a life-long study of "moral insanity," a condition wherein there is complete mental and moral insensitivity, described many cases in which those poor creatures were unable to feel any physical pain at all, even when they were cut with knives or their teeth were drawn without anaesthetic.

On the other hand, in Christ Our Lord, the perfection of manhood, we find the oneness of spirit, mind and body in perfection. Thus in the agony of the garden, when Christ's human intellect was faced with the guilt and suffering of the world, he said, "My soul is ready to die with sorrow" (Matt. xxvi.38), and this sorrow and fear overwhelmed his sacred body, causing the sweat as of blood.

It is only in perfectly integrated manhood that such unity as that can be experienced. We are very far from having the perfect will of Christ which harmonizes every part of human nature and makes the body the perfect expression of the spirit.

We do not realize our unity even though it is a fact. Sometimes we are so conscious of the mental suffering that it seems to have numbed the physical; at other times, this far more often, the bodily side obsesses us to the extinction of our consciousness of all else.

Our bodies play an enormously important part in our life in the Risen Christ. The Incarnation has given a sacramental quality to our flesh and blood, so that we can offer an unceasing prayer of the body, which can begin here and never end, sanctifying not only the suffering of the body but its joys too, in preparation for the eternity when our bodies, which are now all too often a drag upon us, will be glorified as the Risen Body of Christ is now.

When Christ rose from the dead, he rose with the same body that had grown in his mother's womb, shivered in Bethlehem, laboured in Nazareth, fasted in the wilderness. The body which had hungered and thirsted and slept, which had been wounded and suffered and died, the same body, too, that he had taken into his hands and given to us in the breaking of bread at the Last Supper.

About all this he left us no possible doubt. Had he been only a ghost it would have been unnecessary, even absurd, to have told Mary Magdalene not to touch him, and equally without meaning to have taken the hand of the still hesitating Thomas and thrust it into the very wounds of the crucifixion.

But Christ was not content only to prove the reality of his Risen Body, he wanted, during the forty days between the Resurrection and the Ascension, to teach us the mystery of our own prayer of the body in our life in him—to teach us how this prayer was to be made, not only in extraordinary things but every day, in all the ordinary things inseparable from our bodies, their necessities, their limitations, their temptations, their labours and their joys. Christ need not have eaten in his Risen Body—a glorified body does not require food—but to stress the simplicity of our prayer he did eat. Moreover, to show us again that our bodies were to be sanctified by his sacramental body he again broke the bread and gave it to his wondering disciples.

When we are young, in the full vigour of love, the prayer of the body is a thing of delight, like a spontaneous cry of joy to God. It is full of the sweetness of living, of the potentiality of pure love, of responses to the sun and light and darkness, as vibrant and mysterious and sweet as those of the seed in the earth or the sap in the tree. Our strength, our sense of well-being, is something like a shout of praise to God, our five senses like five angels bringing us the messages of his love with touches and tongues of fire. There is something bracing and invigorating even in its inevitable wrestling with temptation and its fasts, while the sacrifice of self sometimes involved in the part it plays in the living out of love touches glory.

For small children things are simpler yet; they derive enormous pleasure from jumping about and turning somersaults and hearing their own voices repeating nonsense words. Such things give them possibilities of prayer and praise as true and lovely as that of the tumbler of Notre Dame.

As time passes, when we get older, or if we fall ill, or even more if we gather to ourselves the little crop of ailments that are part of the fair wear-and-tear of life, we require more discipline, and of a different kind. Before, it was to restrain; now it is time to invigorate or, as we more often *feel*, to *drive*, though in reality the discipline we must use now is, if it is to be effective, so gentle that it brings tranquillity. Prayer, which once did inspire us and give meaning to the tedious things of every day, becomes so irksome in itself that we are hard-pressed to be faithful even to its formal expression. We go on repeating to ourselves that work is prayer, but something has happened to us which makes us feel that in *our* work there is very little prayer and a very great deal of boredom.

It is time to think about the part which the body

has taken in Christ's prayer in his Church for the last two thousand years: I mean in the Liturgy.

The Liturgy is the expression of Christ's love, his prayer in his Mystical Body, into which our own prayer is gathered and integrated. It is not subject, as our personal prayer is, to moods. It never fails, day after day from the rising of the sun to its setting, in age after age, to adore God, to express sorrow for sin, to praise and thank God, to offer sacrifice, to petition for peace. It is the perfect expression of every individual, the voice of the inarticulate lifted in a hymn of love. At the same time it is the chorus of the whole human race made one in communion with Christ.

This supreme prayer is made by body and soul, and the part of the body is not merely an outward formality or symbol, it is integral. The priest who represents all the people in the Liturgy is consecrated to God; his hands in particular are consecrated. Every movement, every gesture, every step he takes in the sanctuary, every word he utters, is preordained by Christ to be the fitting expression of his prayer. Generations of men have learnt to make exactly the same grave, beautiful movements, to utter precisely the same unaltering, effective words, with the same intonations.

The Prayer of the Body

Every word, every movement is effective, every one is a bodily act, and the very changing of the bread and wine into the Body and Blood of Christ is accomplished, because he wills it so, by certain movements and spoken words.

The priest at the altar is not asked to feel any sweetness, to pass into ecstasy, to weep for sin; he is not asked to express his own feelings or fervour; he is not asked to do what no man could do by himself, namely to sustain the sweetness of contact with Heaven all through this life, to realize the horror of sin and experience the fullest felt sorrow for it unceasingly. No, he is asked to put himself aside, and to let Christ in him rejoice and sorrow and pray, and so let the experience of the whole world be his prayer. He stands there as a Christ before God, and the unchanging necessities of the universal adoration of mankind pass through him. He is asked only to surrender his will to Christ, lending his body to those slow, beautiful acts, his tongue to those miraculous words.

The prayer of the Body gathers all our own actions and words and all that we experience with our bodies to this prayer of Christ, if we deliberately impose upon ourselves the same kind of training and discipline that the priest has undergone in order to go into the holy of holies and offer Christ to God in his own poor consecrated hands of flesh and blood.

At the *Orate Fratres*, a little while before the Consecration, the priest makes a complete circle; with extended hands he turns to the people and then right round to the altar. In this complete circle we are gathered into our participation in the Mass, literally into the offering of self, to be made one with the Host.

The offering of the body in this prayer that is at the heart of life includes everything in our daily life, so that from the altar it radiates out into the world we live in, giving the majesty of the liturgical action to our work and leisure, our eating and sleeping and speaking and moving; giving to our simplest act the redeeming power of the offering of Christ's Body, and making it both sacrifice to God and communion with man.

We begin the lesson before the altar, and the first lesson is to be rid of anxiety about our fervour, our failure, our personal intention, our self—to give ourselves up through Christ's words and Christ's gestures to Christ's intentions and desires.

This can begin simply by making the sign of the

cross at the beginning of Mass as slowly and widely as the priest is doing at the foot of the altar. We lift our hand, we make a gesture in the power of the Trinity. Then, not troubling about what we feel, what we fret for, we put into our kneeling and standing and sitting all the majesty, all the obedience, all the simplicity that we can. That is all.

We shall carry this idea into the world, into the kitchen and the office, making life a liturgy, so that through it those prayers that Christ wishes to be made unceasingly will be made, regardless of our mood and in tranquillity.

Now it will be in the power of the Trinity and the majesty of the Liturgy that we do the things which before seemed only effort and boredom. Every step to the office, or to and fro in the home, will be a counted, preordained step, like the numbered steps in the sanctuary. We shall kneel in sorrow for sin and in adoration, whether we kneel to scrub the floor or to fasten the little child's shoe.

In its simplest terms the way to restore our souls in this prayer of the Body is to slow down our pace to the pace of the Liturgy, to prune our minds to its huge simplicities.

This, starkly simple though it is, is a life's work. It cannot be said that a stranger visiting a Catholic church would immediately observe the beautiful, disciplined movements of the celebrant repeated by the whole congregation. On the contrary, he might reasonably suppose that a plague of flies swarmed from the holy-water stoup which the faithful were trying to brush away from their noses; and a young child who asked whether it were correct to genuflect *after* Mass "at the run" was being not impertinent but observant.

Before Christ died he literally gave us his sacramental body in his own hands. Day after day he is born in the consecrated hands of the priest; in a man's hands he is lifted up and offers himself to the Father. It is fitting, then, that so often our offering of self through the body must be made literally with our hands.

What an expression of himself a man's hands are. When he comes to die, what a story his hands tell. They have taken on the shape and colour and texture of his work. They are the story of his life. When Madame Curie lay dead, the most beautiful testimonial to her life's work was in her hands lying simply on the coverlet, scarred with burns of radium.

The Prayer of the Body

Long before Christ gave us his body in his own hands they were hardened by toil, beautiful with the line and muscle and sinew of the hands of an artisan, and hollowed out by the wooden mallet to cup the chalice and hold the nail. But in the consummation of his self-giving, these hands which had given in so many ways were helpless, fastened back, immovable, to a plank.

At that moment his body was broken, the heart was broken, the flesh and blood separated. Every day the suffering of the Lord's body is shown in the breaking of the bread.

Sooner or later, our prayer of the body too becomes the helpless hands, the falling away of self, the breaking of the bread. Sickness, old age, death; these must come, and when they come it seems that our service is ended. There is exhaustion which makes it first an effort, then an impossibility, to lift the hand up to make the sign of the cross; no more liturgical acts in daily life, gestures and symbols that worship God and give Christ's love to men.

Everything falls away from us, even memories—even the weariness of self. This is the breaking of the bread, the supreme moment in the prayer of the body, the end of the liturgy of our mortal lives, when we are broken for and in the communion of Christ's love to the whole world.

But it is not the end of the prayer of the body. To that there is no end. Our dust pays homage to God, until the endless morning of resurrection wakens our body, glorified.

CHAPTER SEVEN

WORK

At first sight is seems strange to include a chapter on work in meditations on the Risen Christ.

We have come to think of work almost with shrinking. Many of us think of it simply as overwork, as working against time, a habit which is all too often a necessity, which, if it be brain work, so blunts the mind in the end that it spoils everything it attempts, and becomes like a blunted and jagged instrument in the hand of a surgeon.

Or, if we think of manual labour, we call up a dark picture of industrial abuses, exploitation, black factory

towns under palls of smoke, wretched slums strag-
gling round coal mines or docks; and following this
another picture, which, if outwardly less tragic, is inwardly even more so. We see the workers regimented
into strikers, their hardships exploited, their feelings
aggravated by those who outrage them even more,
because they manage to instil a wholly and solely material ideal, to twist the worker's sense of justice into
a thirst for vengeance and to convince him that en-
mity between different groups of men is so inevitable
that it may almost be regarded as natural law!

Another kind of work which calls up a dreary picture is woman's work in the home. It is true that many
magazine articles paint this in rosy colours and that
many unmarried girls who read them think that they
would be happy working in a home of their own.
Sometimes they are; more often they merely think
the drudgery is worth while. If they love their husband and their children, it is worth while to face the
monotony every morning and the weariness every
night; but that is a very far cry indeed from finding
their work, in itself, a source of real happiness. Again,
more and more women prefer to go out to work in an
office in order to be able to pay someone else to look

after their children and to clean the house. Among those who cannot escape in this way, there is a dreadful minority of depressed and depressing wives and mothers, who half-do all that they do, who wait the homecoming of the family only to have an audience for their martyrdom.

Turning from these dreary pictures of work to the thought of the Resurrection is like walking out of a thick grey fog into the transparent sunlight of early morning. It is turning from men heavy with care and menacing to one another, to a man who comes towards us radiant, not only from the stone tomb, but from the captivity of all human affliction.

Everything is lyrical; no matter if cynics think this sentimental, we cannot think of the Resurrection and not think of flowers opening shadowless faces to a new dawn, of their green leaves saturated by the light of the rising sun, of the miracle of the first bird song, of the awakening of all that slept, the rebirth into light of all that was in darkness. When we look back across the two thousand years to the then, which faith tells us is also the now, we see that first step of the Risen Lord upon the earth in the footprint that shines in the morning dew. If there is any sighing at all, audible in that quiet garden, it is the sigh of ineffable love breathed by the Holy Spirit, when the first beat of the human heart of the Son worships the Father again.

What connection is there between these two men, the sombre, menacing worker of today, and the radiant young man in the garden of tombs, whose every heart-beat renews the love dormant in all men?

The answer is that the Christ who lives on in the life of every worker is potentially that same Christ who rises daily, hourly from the dead; potentially at least in every worker is the joyful Son of God, to whom all work was, and is, what God intended it to be, adoration or contemplation that makes all things new.

If we have so smudged and bleared God's image in us that even when our souls are not quite dead, we can no longer recognize Christ in them, this is in great measure due to our complete misconception of work.

Work is intended to be a thing which restores God's image in us—not, as we have ourselves made it, something which effaces it, and with it almost effaces our humanity.

At the root of our false conception is the idea that

work is simply a punishment for sin. If Adam had not sinned, we imagine that we should all be idle, and strange as this is, many of us think that being idle is being happy.

The fact is that work was intended by God to be one of the joys of the Garden of Eden. Adam, and his children, were to *work* in the garden: "And God pronounced his blessing on them, Increase and multiply and fill the earth, and make it yours" (Gen. i.28). And again: ". . . the Lord God took the man and put him in his garden of delight, to cultivate and tend it" (Gen. ii.15).

So it is evident that before Adam sinned, therefore before there was any suffering, Adam was intended to work, and since in Eden the whole joy that man was made for was to know and love God, work must have been one of the ways of knowing him, a means of blissful contemplation.

After all, if man was made in God's image, and God rejoiced in creating the world, is it not logical that he should will that man, whom he so loved, should be allowed, for his own delight, to share in the creation?

No doubt there was a first autumn and a first winter

in Eden, and then a first spring. Only, in that first winter there would have been the wonder of the sheer loveliness of snow, with its deep silence and purity of whiteness, and of the myriad sparkling snowflakes; but no suffering and perishing from cold for the little animals in Adam's care, nothing lost or frightened or homeless. And then, when spring came, imagine the amazement and enthralling wonder in the heart of the first man when he saw the first seed that he had sown pierce the ground, and, suddenly, all the wild green loveliness of creation flowed from his own fingertips! Work was not the punishment for sin; but the suffering that complicated work, after the Fall, was and still is the punishment.

In the heart of man, an essential part of his likeness to God is this, he is a maker. God made everything; man, if he is to be happy, like God, must make something. He reflects his Creator. He must make something which he has conceived in his own mind and which he longs to see, to be able to touch and hold, something that will have substance and shape and purpose, that will be outside of himself, and yet will remain, as an idea, in himself.

In this kind of making man comes to know God, not

from what anyone outside tells him, but from himself; he learns his Creator's joy from the joy in his own, the maker's heart.

The tragedy of the modern world is that the idea of being a maker is almost forgotten. If men at work make anything at all now, it is not anything conceived within themselves, neither do they make anything wholly by themselves, so that they can feel it to be part of themselves—"The Word" (in their own souls) "made flesh."

Most workers who make anything concrete at all make only a fraction of something, which is not only not their own conception, but which they may never even see completed. Again, even the man who conceived it seldom did so because it expressed the beauty or the love in his own soul, but only for the money it would bring to him.

Perhaps the only kind of man who still experiences the joy that work should be is the artist, and even then only the artist who has almost miraculously preserved his integrity. Such an artist is seldom looked to by so-called normal men for an example, because they regard him as a madman. Rather than do what they consider to be a respectable job, that is, a job that he does not want to do, he is willing to be poor, to be cold and hungry. Moreover, they think that he contributes nothing to society, for few men would think that a poem or a picture or a carving contributes anything. Indeed, it is the exceptional work of art that is a real gift to the world, but the artist contributes a great deal more than his work of art. He keeps alive the idea of work as a joy in itself; even when he is ignorant of what prayer means theologically, in him the idea of work as prayer is manifest.

Do not imagine that I am going to suggest either that everyone should try to get round the dilemma by a spare-time hobby, or that we should all set our faces against progress and insist upon homemade whole-meal bread, home-woven clothes that hang like bags of sackcloth, pots from our own potter's wheel, and so on. On the contrary, it seems to me that those who live the Christ-life must keep the artist's *ideal* always before them, even in their lives as they are now. They must regard themselves, not first of all as workers, but as makers, even as co-makers with God. This will apply to every one, from a company director to the smallest factory girl, and it will include everyone— the city workers, the farmers and labourers, the

women in the home, the nurses and doctors and law-
yers, and the children doing their lessons at school.

If we ask *why* God made animals and flowers and
all the amazing variety of things that he did; why he
made winds that would move so fast and so far; why
he made movement itself; why indeed he made all
that is, and even the power in man's mind and the
impulse to make the things that man makes; the
answer is, simply for love.

In the ideal artist, fashioning with his hands from
some substance outside himself that which is in his
heart—so that he can take it into his hands and, looking on it, look on the image and likeness of his inmost,
invisible self—we have an image of the Blessed
Trinity.

The whole world was created because of the love
between the three Persons of the Blessed Trinity; the
earth was created to be the womb and the cradle of
Christ. Every human being was, in the Creator's love,
"another Christ." When the Spirit breathed upon the
waters, the breath was the sighing of utter love of the
Holy Spirit; when God said "Let there be light" the
light was the shadow of that Light which was to shine
in darkness, already the radiance of his Eternal Light.

The meaning of Creation is love; God created for love, and what he created *is* love.

It is this part of the mystery that should reform our idea of work. We cannot all make works of art in the narrow sense, but we can all be artists and creators: in our attitude to our work we can make what we make *first of all for love*.

Suppose the man at the head of a business makes a plan, he can make it first of all for the good of everyone concerned. Suppose a boy in the workroom makes a screw, he can put the best in him into the making, because he is doing it as his own part in the common good. If a woman makes a pudding, she tries to make it as good a pudding as she can, not for the love of puddings but for the love of the man and the children to be nourished by it. Suppose the husband makes a balance sheet at the office, he makes it as good and right a balance sheet as he can, less because he loves mathematical precision and order, than because he is working for the well-being of his family.

We use the expression to "make love," but limit it to one idea. The whole life of every worker should *make* love. All work should be an act of creative love.

It is obvious that even with this ideal before him,

the man who lives in Christ will have much bitterness
to overcome. The fact that he begins to make his
balance sheet a thing of beauty, or to work his lathe
as lovingly as he would have sharpened a saw in
Nazareth, will not necessarily convert the bank manager to his views; he will still have the heartbreak
of having to work in circumstances frustrating to the
beauty of his own work. Likewise the fact that a
manager or owner or even a company director comes
to think of making a plan for his industry as really
making something for the love of mankind, will not
cause those who are to carry out his plan to believe
in him, or to give up their own adherence to a purely
material ideal. The director is as likely as the least of
his workers to be faced with mistrust and cynicism.

But each individual who does renew his own spirit
to work with this ideal does do something; in fact, he
does a great deal to bring about the reform of the
world's work, which is a basic necessity for human
happiness, and this because no one can have this idea
of work without getting some joy out of his own work,
and, if thought is not *always* infectious, joy is. But
before all else, when work becomes contemplation,
man learns to know the joy of the love of the Blessed

Trinity through his own experience; learns it from his own heart, making his own world one in which Christ is made new. He possesses himself of the inexpressible mystery of the Creator's joy in making a new world that is to cradle Christ.

CHAPTER EIGHT

THE CROWN OF THORNS

Every young Catholic child learns to repeat that "prayer is the raising of the heart and mind to God," and usually the catechist stresses the fact that the heart is the most important.

This warning is quite unnecessary, as most people, young and old alike, find it fairly easy to raise the heart to God, but almost impossible to raise the mind.

There are several main reasons for this. One is that there is a type of amiable congenital density which has been unofficially canonized by a powerful minority of Catholics.

In the Middle Ages mental deficients were almost venerated. That is beautiful and right; poor little mentally deficient children are thought to be protected by their disability; they never cease to be children and never lose their innocence and therefore have a very special place in the Heavenly Father's heart.

To some extent ordinarily stupid people may be said to be protected too; they seldom excel in repartee, and so seldom have sharp tongues; they are saved many pitfalls by the slowness of their thinking. They seldom have any critical faculty and consequently are not tempted to judge others; here again they are spared one of the most persistent temptations. They are not only very easily exploited, but so little are they able to realize this that they are beamingly grateful for the patronage they win by doing all the unpleasant, dull tasks, and consequently they are often very popular.

It is not surprising, then, that stupidity is very often confused with holiness and flatteringly but wrongly described as simplicity.

Just as stupidity is thought safe, it is thought dangerous by the timider kind of authority to be clever, and it seldom occurs to teachers that it is not necessary to be clever to think, and quite often clever people do not.

It is true that a clever person has a harder path to travel, one beset with temptations; he is likely to be more interested in people, therefore more critical and more analytical and probably more extreme in his likes and dislikes; but since no one is safe who is not consciously at war with himself, such temptations, and indeed all temptations, may be considered not as a stumbling-block but as a grace.

Thinking, however, is not the prerogative of clever people; it is something which everyone (even stupid people) could do if he tried, and which everyone has an obligation to try to do.

As for thinking about God—this can *begin* by thinking about the least thing God has made and all it tells us about God. Blessed Juliana of Norwich started by thinking about an acorn; one could even start by thinking about a toad.

We are constantly told that "Catholics are not allowed to think," and the strange, tragic thing is that there are many people outside the Church today because they believe it, and presumably many Catholics fail to disillusion them. At the same time, if they are challenged, it transpires that though they are *allowed* to think, they don't, and don't want to; and should they encounter the formidable Catholic who does think, and who offers them, let us say, the Blessed Trinity to start thinking about, they hastily retire, and take cover under the plea that they are "only a very simple person."

Another reason why the *mind* is seldom raised to God is because nine out of ten people are unable to use their minds at all, or at all events to concentrate them at all on the invisible world.

We live in the midst of incessant noise, which curiously enough is the only environmental condition to which, it has been scientifically proved, human nature does not and cannot adapt itself. One becomes unconscious of part of the noise, but nevertheless the tension is going on. All the amusements and comforts of modern civilization destroy thought; the radio must always be on, for one member of the family or another always wants something that the others do not, and if there happens to be a real enthusiast in the family, he will certainly want to tune in to every station in the world for hours on end, not listening to any programme anywhere, but filling the house with crackles and shrieks and groans as he moves across the world.

Now television threatens the remnants of sanity. Some families sit in the dark to look at it every night, and with drawn blinds by day, and there see in a reduced scale the day's sport, or something equally stimulating to the mind. The entertainment which modern science brings into the home might be less intolerable were it not that in any case most homes today are already overcrowded, which in itself is a source of irritability and constant distraction.

Speed too is a difficulty, if only because almost the only time that most people have for reading is when they are travelling, and travelling takes less and less time. Worse still, people are usually working against time, and fatigue adds to the difficulty of thinking and reading.

There is another very big cause of our unthinking, and that is a certain kind of sentimentality, or inability to face facts. Thinking involves us in the necessity of looking some hard facts straight in the face: evil, suffering, the apparent injustice of life, death.

Now a very great number of people are turning

away from these things, not because they really think that they are unreal, or that any beautiful theory or homemade spirituality could make them any pleasanter, but simply because they *have* been face to face with them, too close to them, and they are sickened by them.

It is impossible for anyone to have been in the heart of a war such as we have known, to have seen the cruelty and tragedy of it stripped naked, to have been obliged literally to handle it, to embrace it, to make it one's daily and nightly life for years, and not to be at the same time convinced of the reality of evil and its results, and so sickened by both that even the most ludicrous wishful unthinking is preferable to having to remind ourselves of it all, by thinking out the theological explanations.

But a Christian is bound to think; he owes it to God, and he owes it to the world. He is bound to think about these hard facts as well as the lovely things in life, because he is here precisely for one purpose, to lead the Risen Life of Christ, who has overcome the world.

Christ described himself and his apostles by exactly the same symbol, light. "I am the light of the world, he said. He who follows me can never walk in darkness" (John viii.12); and to his apostles through the ages: "You are the light of the world. . . . A lamp is not lighted to be put away under a bushel measure; it is put on the lamp-stand, to give light to all the people of the house; and your light must shine so brightly before men that they can see your good works, and glorify your Father who is in heaven" (Matt. v.14-16). These two sayings taken together are a wonderful testimony to the identification of the Christian with Christ.

Christ does not say "I am the light of the world, which you must reflect," but that both he and we *are* the identical light, the light of the world.

We are not only given the hands of Christ to work with, and the heart of Christ to love with, but the mind of Christ to illuminate the world with. His plan of love is consistent through and through; through our personal lives we are to give his love to one another, through the sacraments we are to give his life to one another, through his light in us, we are to give his mind to one another.

This means first of all that we are to see everything in life as he sees it, with his mind, through his eyes, in his light. But we shall have to think, mentally to wrestle with the angel, to come to this illumination of our own thought. Because Christ sees everything from a totally different point of view to that of materialist man. Everything that we see as a curse he saw as a blessing: poverty, being exploited and tried, mourning, being persecuted and reviled, all these things are blessed in his eyes. He saw his own Passion as the time of his glory, and so of his Father's glory. And Christ not only speaks and thinks truly, he is truth itself.

The man who lives in Christ must learn to see the real meaning of suffering; he must accept the fact that it has been caused by man's sin, and that it is man who has laid the burden of it on Christ, so that now to be one with Christ means that we must, personally, accept the responsibility of the sins of the world.

It is man who crowned Christ with thorns, and the man who is one with Christ must necessarily wear his crown.

If anyone does see with Christ's eyes, he will learn that there is glory in suffering, because Christ has transformed it and given it the power of his love; therefore that which once destroyed, now mends and heals. Every jot of human suffering borne with the fortitude and love of Christ reduces the burden of all mankind, destroys a jot of sin with its evil power to hurt, and does glorify God.

Again, we are not told by Christ to think only about stark and terrible things, but about the little and lovely and happy things all round us. We are usually so preoccupied with anxiety that we hardly see them at all, and so intent upon racing time that we certainly never stop to contemplate them and to think about them. Wild flowers, birds, wheat growing in the countryside. Christ himself evidently thought about everything, and saw in everything an example or a symbol of his Father's love: the bread rising in the oven, the bottling of wine, even women mending clothes, were sufficient things for Christ to think about, and his thought was a great procession of light, kindled by a spark from that tiny detail of domestic life, or by a gust of wind or a flower, or a bird crossing heaven, to sweep up on a great arc to the Father's throne and thence to encircle the world.

Light—what a lovely thing that is, which we are told we *are*. It enables people to see things distinctly and as what they are. "Let us have light," said Victor

Hugo. "Light in floods; bats cannot face the dawn!"

It warms, it heals, it penetrates, it gives life, it gives colour and beauty to everything that it touches. It is the light of the sun that renews the earth; it was the light of a star that proclaimed Christ's birth.

It is light that guides ships to safety through deep seas, light that welcomes us from far off from the window of home: and it is the humble light of home that Christ speaks of first of all when he tells us we are the light of the world.

It is first of all in the home that the light of Christ must shine from our minds.

It is in the home, where we are over-familiar with the simplicities that ought to lift our heart and *mind* to God, and where suffering, because it is our own or, worse still, our children's, is hard to see in the sense of glory, or to welcome, even though it may start the world's healing.

There are parents belonging to the school of escape through whimsical unthinking who deliberately teach their little children that there is no such thing as death; while others, realizing how soon life will call their bluff, say that everyone, no matter what kind of life he has lived on earth, goes straight to Heaven.

As to teaching their over-protected children that they too are little Christs and can also enter into his glory by their small sacrifices, they do all that they can to encourage them in selfishness and self-indulgence—and these are the children who are to go out into the world as it is today, as Christs, to bring light and savour, joy and beauty and comfort and love to suffering humanity!

Those who are one with Christ, who do see with his vision and insight, look at everything from the point of view of our Heavenly Father, not only because he is omnipotent—that would not move pigmy men—but because his love for us, rightly understood, is the only real and lasting source of our delight, the only thing that can reconcile us to our suffering, and the only thing that can overcome the fears and the gnawing anxieties which beset us.

This was Christ's motive in all his thinking; he did not point to flowers and birds only because they are intrinsically lovely, but because if we would only begin to *think*, we would come to the inevitable conclusion that we are far more dear to God than they are, and can trust him unhesitatingly for all that we need.

When he foretold his Passion, he did not dwell upon the horror of it, but spoke at once of what hope and life it would bring to the world—the resurrection that would go on through the ages, and of how the crucifixion would draw all men to the heart of redeeming love.

Now, to think with Christ's mind is not easy; it means that we must study theology at least as eagerly as we study the cookery book, that we must learn enough inward recollection to be able to think in the midst of chaos—in the street—in the family; that we must wrest the secret of God from every trifle and have the courage to see it in the immensities of sorrow.

Thinking with Christ's mind today is, as it was two thousand years ago, putting on the crown of thorns. The mind will be wounded, will suffer, will labour in thought again—but the mind will be crowned. And when the light of the world dawns in the darkness within the thorn-bound, bowing head of the Christman today, and shines out from it like the rising sun, waking the world from the dreams of the night to the reality of the morning, then he who wears it will be able to cry out exultantly with the Russian poet Nekrasov:

". . . there are times, there are ages,
when nothing is more desirable,
nothing more beautiful than the crown of thorns."

CHAPTER NINE

REST

Man's Christ-life on earth is not an easy life. It is a cowardly as well as a stupid thing to try to approach it as if it were. It is a joyful life, however, which is a very different thing, and sometimes we are apt to forget that joy is the predominating thing in the Christ-life. We forget this, because it is so necessary to stress the other side, the part that sorrow and hardship play, and the glorious fact of Christ's Passion going on in men today.

The dark side, or the *seemingly* dark side, must be dwelt on, because the world is obsessed by suffering, and everyone who thinks at all asks, and has a perfect right to ask, what all this suffering means, what purpose, if any, does it serve, why is it allowed? Questions which can only be answered in the light of Christ's coming to earth to take the burden of man's sin upon himself, and living on in men, that they might take the glory of his redeeming love to be their own.

But we should not forget that Christ did not bring the suffering of his Passion to us; he brought his infinite love to us, it is we who gave the suffering to *him*. He gives suffering the power of his love, and, therefore, when we accept the suffering necessarily involved in living the Christ-life in this world, we are not submerging ourselves more deeply into suffering than we need have done, but are doing something which will transform it ultimately into joy.

There is a certain kind of spirituality which seems to ignore this, and to forget Christ's own words, spoken just before his Passion: "All this I have told you, so that my joy may be yours, and the measure of your joy may be filled up" (John xv.11). Those who practise this spirituality seem to think that a constant morbid dwelling on suffering and a joyless life of austerity and drabness is a real imitation of Christ.

Their attitude to Christianity is not one of acceptance but of insistence, insistence on something that is false.

This would be a sad thing for the individuals themselves even if they were responsible only to themselves, but every Christian is responsible to every other, to give Christ's love, to radiate his light, to fill up the measure of his joy. It is those people who insist upon this gloomy negative kind of spirituality, especially when it is accompanied by a restless zeal, who drive young people away from religion. The reasons are obvious.

The Christ-life is a joyful one, but it is hard, it is not easy, because it is never for one moment the line of least resistance; it is a continual conquest. The non-Christian of the post-Christian world, often a charming and amiable person, can rid himself of the agony of temptation simply by giving way to it; the Christian has to go on wrestling with it, and to go on feeling the agony of it while he does so. The non-Christian can get round the difficulties and sacrifices involved in living a family life and an honest life in a world of materialism, but the Christian cannot, he can never get round anything, he has to square his shoulders, face the difficulties and make the sacrifices involved in daily life, and he has to go on loving those who have made his daily life literally a taking up the cross daily.

For such conquest, it is necessary for the Christian to be constantly made new, reinvigorated; and for this two things are vital: one, that he will brace himself, soul and body, for the fight; and the other, in a sense the opposite, that he will relax, that he will lay open his heart and mind to *receive* the flood of joy and light God is always pouring into it, so that his Christ-life may be the glad thing of glory and love it is intended to be.

This brings us to that often neglected thing, so essential to our life in the Risen Christ, and so often neglected or even, by the gloomy zealots, repudiated: rest.

In thinking of the Christ-life, we have dwelt on practical, often material, things and given little thought to the invisible things of mind and spirit. These things of mind and spirit give joy and give the sacramental touch to the material life which transforms it. They depend upon the descent of the Holy Ghost into our souls.

If we turn for a moment to the child's catechism

and think what the "gifts and fruits" of the Holy Ghost listed there are, we can see at once why the inflowing of the Spirit of God gives joy to men even in the midst of suffering and hardship: peace, patience, fortitude, wisdom, understanding, joy itself!

Or turn to the lovely hymn for the Feast of Pentecost in the Missal to see what the Holy Ghost is to man, and what the descent of the Holy Ghost into his soul does to him.

He is the comforter, that is the one who makes strong; he is rest in toil, shade and refreshment in the heat of noon, solace in grief. He is the light of our life, the light that shines in our darkness.

It is the Holy Ghost, so this hymn goes on to tell us, who washes away the stains of our sins; the exquisite quality of water recurs again and again, to quench our thirst; "the pilgrim's sweet relief" to wash away our stains of sin, and to "water from Heaven our barren clay"—to come down into the dried-up, arid life and water it as the blessed rain waters the parched earth, giving life to the seed in it, causing a new spring to break from it in all its cool and overflowing loveliness of green bud and leaf. In our souls this is a new springtide of Christ, an answer to the age-long prayer "Let the earth be opened and bud forth a saviour."

And not only does the Holy Spirit wash the stains from our souls and our minds, but he heals the wounds and bruises of life, he softens the pride that is so often the major cause of our unhappiness, and bows our "stiff necks" to the yoke that is sweet and brings us peace. He warms the hearts that had grown cold and makes them human again, tender to one another, loving towards God, capable once again of bringing more to the measure of love, which is the hope of the world. He recalls us to the Source to drink, to the Source of our life and joy, and all this is not simply to brace us for conquest and to enable us to suffer here, it is to flood all suffering here with joy, and finally to flood death itself with peace and to bring us to the final realization of joy which will never end.

> "Grant us in life thy grace that we
> In peace may die and ever be
> In joy before thy face."

This Pentecost hymn not only points to *why* the Holy Ghost makes this life joyful, but to the fact that rest is the right preparation for the descent of the Holy Ghost: and why.

It shows us too what the nature of this supernatural rest is to be, and why.

The Christ-life in us follows a natural law of growth. All nature is made in the image of Christ's life, and Christ chose to submit himself to his own law; he was hidden in his Mother's womb, like a seed in the earth, and there grew towards his birth. Our Lady could do nothing to hurry that birth, and she would not have wished to. She rested in God's will, in his timing, his planning; her mind was as big as the earth, as peaceful as the earth, as still as the earth in winter, and it covered Heaven—Heaven unfelt yet, unseen, growing towards the birth of Christ.

Now most of us tend to want to *feel* the presence of the indwelling Christ all the time; we want to experience continual sweetness in devotion, our prayers are to be always breaking into flower within us, we are distressed because we know long periods when prayer brings *us* no sweetness at all, and we forget in our distress that if we go on praying without any "consolation," we are giving *God* something due to him.

We are impatient because we do not immediately *feel* the healing of our wounds, or do not at once after confession recover from the effects of our sins; we are still tempted, and if we have formed a bad habit, it will take *time* to unform it.

The beginning of the rest which will allow the Holy Ghost to flood our souls consists in accepting God's plan, and in that plan there is winter as well as spring, spring as well as summer with its flowering, and autumn with its harvest. This means that we must deliberately refuse to be anxious. There are times when we shall not *feel* the indwelling of Christ, when we shall not *feel* that we have faith in it even, and these times, blessed winters of the spirit, are the times when Christ is growing in our souls. Again, these times of dryness in prayer; times when, if we are honest, we know that we have not entered into "the dark night of the soul" but have merely become bored by prayer, because being human our emotions move round in great cycles, and after a period of intense sweetness, or of giving out from ourselves to others, a succeeding period of emptiness and flatness is certain: this time of emptiness is the preparation for the new influx of life, the new sweetness, which we cannot force but which will come only when there *is* an empty heart, a fallow mind, waiting the inrush of Heaven's life.

Just as rest means accepting God's plan of our nature and limitations tranquilly, in order that Christ may grow in us and that we may be made new in his way, we must also accept the spring when it comes.

Those gloomy Christians who repudiate joy and dwell *exclusively* on suffering never open their hearts and never let nature empty them ready for the new life to pour in; they refuse to be tranquil in the winter of the soul because they are as avid to *feel* suffering as the others are to feel sweetness, and they mistrust the spring—mistrust the little bud of eternal love in the breaking of its snowy flower and the tenderness of its green leaf!

However, at the present time, rest is not easy for anyone, particularly for those who feel the Kingdom of Christ to be in their keeping on earth. It is difficult for any Christian, faced as he must be with the ever-increasing threat to Christianity, to come to rest, to bring his mind into tranquillity, and to withdraw from time to time; and in these times ordained by God especially, to rest, to trust, to accept.

Too many anxious Christians today think that their efforts to preach and teach and enter into outward activities can do more to save the world than the surrender of their souls to God, to become Christ-bearers.

They believe that they can do more than Our Lady did, and they have no time to stop to consider the absurdity of this. They fear that if the world goes on hurling itself into disaster, as it seems to be doing now, Christ's Kingdom may be defeated. This is not so; Christ has given his word that he will be with, and in, his "little flock" until the end of the world; however dark our days may seem to be for Christianity, they are not so dark as the night following the crucifixion must have seemed to be to the apostles. For that night Christ had already prepared them. He told them to *wait*: to wait for the coming of the Holy Ghost. He told them that he was going away, that they would no longer see him and know the consolation of his presence with them, but that it was better for them that he should go, and that the condition for the coming of the Holy Ghost, through whom he would live on *in* them, was his going: "And yet I can say truly that it is better for you I should go away; he who is to befriend you will not come to you unless

I do go, but if only I make my way there, I will send him to you" (John xvi.7-8).

Christ himself prepared for his Resurrection by resting in the tomb, just as he had prepared for his birth by resting in his mother's womb. He did not call the legions of angels whom he could have called to fight back the forces of evil that had crucified him; he simply lay in the tomb at rest and, at the appointed moment in time, rose from death to renew the life of the whole world.

The apostles, like the modern apostles, were afraid, and with good cause; in spite of their utter failure during the Passion, they, with the Mother of Christ, alone stood for Christ's Kingdom, and the murderous hatred of Christ's enemies pointed straight at them. They shared the reasonable fear of the modern apostle.

But Christ told them simply to wait in the city until the Holy Ghost came to them; not to run away, not to make plans of their own, not to be troubled, either concerning their own recent failure and sin or concerning the danger that fenced them all round, but only to wait, with his mother among them, for the coming of the Comforter who would make them strong, heal their wounds, wash the stains from their souls and be their joy.

"And behold, I am sending down upon you the gift which was promised by my Father; you must wait in the city, until you are clothed with power from on high" (Luke xxiv.49).

Christ does not change, the preparation for the coming of the Spirit is the same today as two thousand years ago, whether it be for the rebirth of Christ in one soul that is in the hard winter, or for the return from the grave of Christ, whose blood is shed again by the martyrs; the preparation is the same, the still, quiet mind, acceptance, and remaining close to the Mother of God, resting in her rest while the life of the world grew within her towards the flowering of everlasting joy.